MOUSETOWN

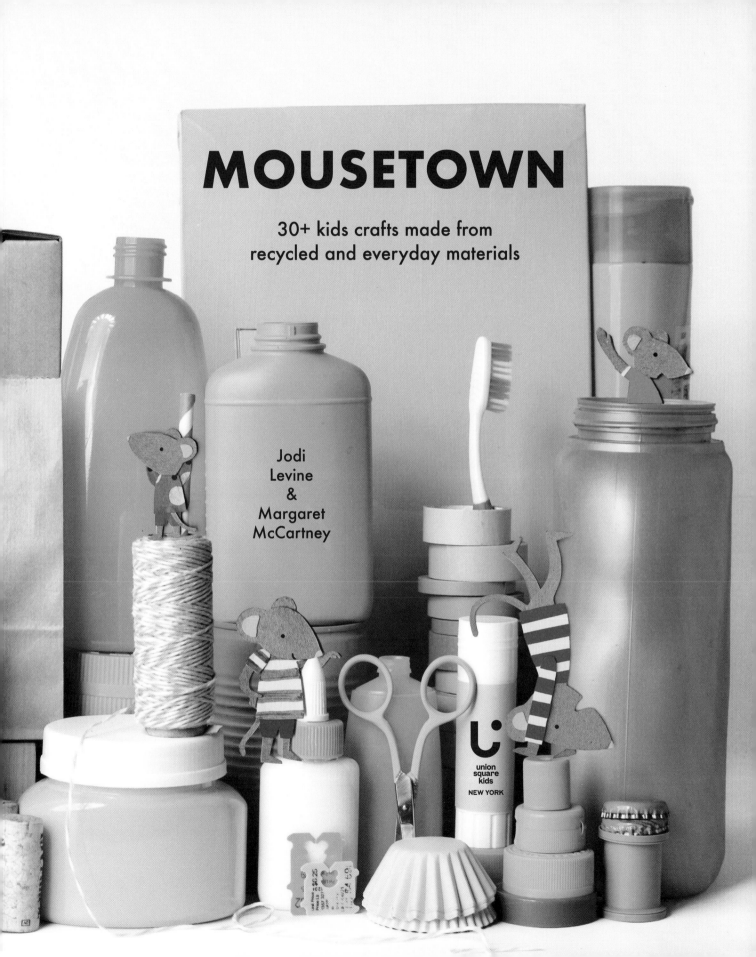

MOUSETOWN

30+ kids crafts made from
recycled and everyday materials

Jodi
Levine
&
Margaret
McCartney

union
square
kids

NEW YORK

for Jeff, Felix, Mom & Dad

for Fred, Sammy, Lionel, Mom & Dad

**union
square
kids**

NEW YORK

UNION SQUARE KIDS and the distinctive Union Square Kids logo are trademarks of Union Square & Co., LLC. Union Square & Co., LLC, is a subsidiary of Sterling Publishing Co., Inc.

This book is intended for young readers with adult supervision only. The publisher has made every effort to ensure that all instructions in this book are accurate, but safety precautions are always recommended when doing crafts and other activities. Adults should use their judgment on the age-appropriateness of activities and should not let children under three years old participate in activities with any small components that could pose a hazard. The publisher shall not be liable or responsible in any respect for any injuries, losses, and/or damages that may result from the use of any information in this book.

ISBN 978-1-4549-5215-2 (paperback)
ISBN 978-1-4549-5216-9 (e-book)

Library of Congress Control Number: 2023038002

For information about custom editions, special sales, and premium purchases, please contact specialsales@unionsquareandco.com.

Printed in China

Lot #: 10 9 8 7 6 5 4 3 2 1

04/24

unionsquareandco.com

Cover and interior design by Jodi Levine & Margaret McCartney

Table of Contents

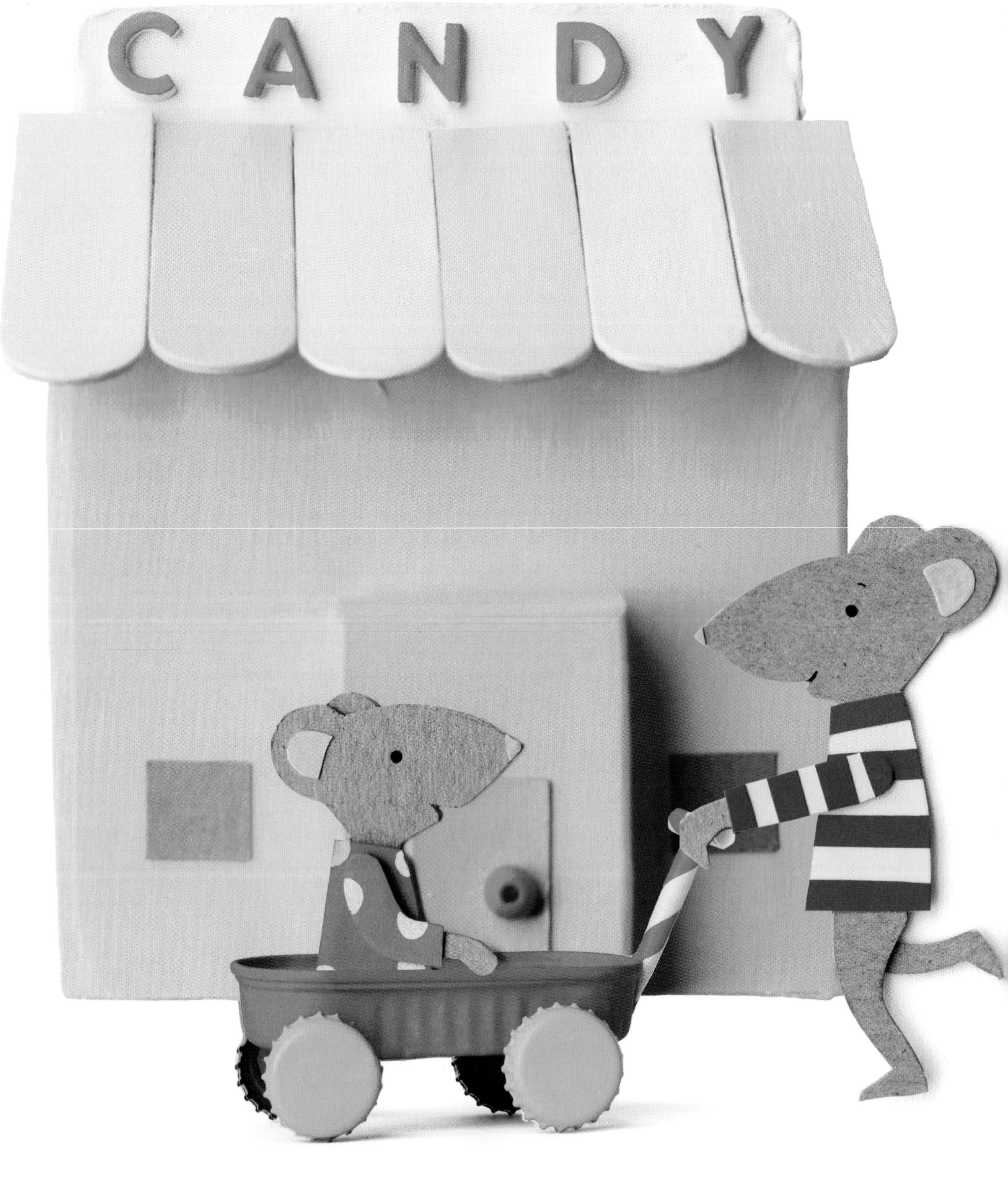
CANDY

Introduction

Welcome to Mousetown! I'm Mouse, and this is my friend Ginger. Follow us from my house to the bakery where we work, and we will teach you how to make the tiniest treats: cakes, pies, and even tiny ice cream cones. You'll make your own Mousetown out of recycled materials too. And I can't wait for you to see the surprise that is coming! For some projects, you need the help of a grown-up mouse, er, person. This symbol lets you know when to ask for help!

See you in Mousetown!

Mouse

Toolbox

*To create your own mini Mousetown,
you will need these tools and supplies.*

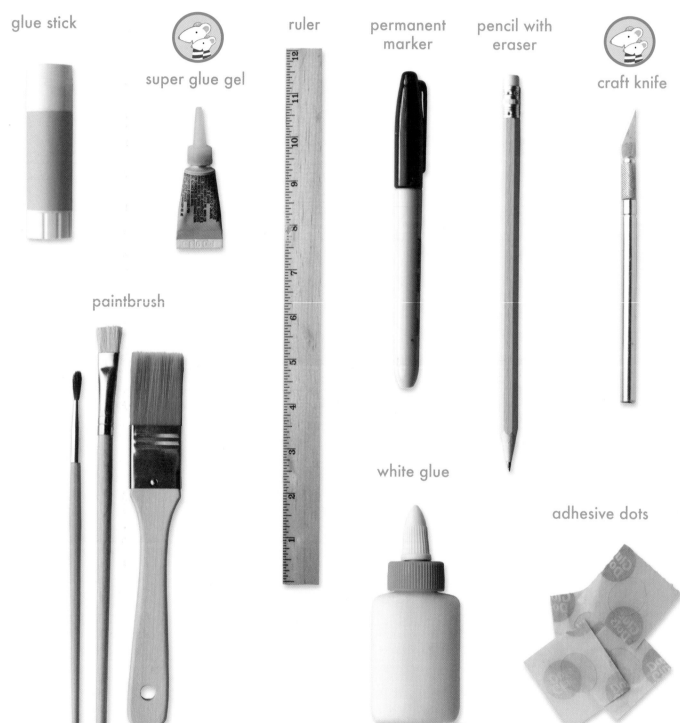

glue stick

super glue gel

ruler

permanent
marker

pencil with
eraser

craft knife

paintbrush

white glue

adhesive dots

scissors

hole punch

toothpicks

clear tape

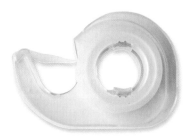

double-sided tape

gesso

acrylic craft paint

washi tape

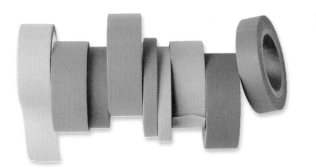

sandpaper

extra supplies to have on hand:

wire cutters
pinking shears
markers
masking tape
string or twine
hot glue gun &
glue sticks
serrated knife

Recycling Bin & Household Materials

*Recycled and household materials are super important for these crafts.
You'll be surprised how much cool stuff you will find around the house.*

paper bags

straws

coffee stirrers

toilet paper tubes

baker's twine

thimbles

Mouse saves this
from bakery boxes!

thin cardboard
(like from cereal boxes)

corrugated
cardboard

scrap paper (newspaper, wrapping
paper, maps, paper bags)

Don't throw away those bottle caps, toilet paper tubes,
or matchboxes—they can all be used right here in Mousetown.
If you love to make things, start collecting items that can
be turned into tiny crafts. Instead of just throwing something
away, reuse it. The best part? It's free!

jar caps

anchovy or sardine tins

cupcake papers

buttons

wire caps

metal bottle caps

small boxes
(raisin boxes, matchboxes)

corks

spools

caps (like from lip
balm, glue stick,
toothpaste)

wooden cheese box lids

Mouse also collects:
• milk cartons in all sizes
• plastic bottles: like shampoo bottles, cold cream jars,
milk jugs, lemon juice bottles
• thin cardboard boxes: spaghetti boxes,
cereal boxes, toothpaste boxes
• clear plastic boxes and lids (like from greens containers)
• clear plastic caps (like from spray pump bottles)

11

Chapter 1:

MOUSE'S

HOUSE

Hey, Mouse! Time to get up. Ginger will be here soon!

Build a Tiny Mousehouse

Every mouse needs a house!

2 half-gallon milk cartons

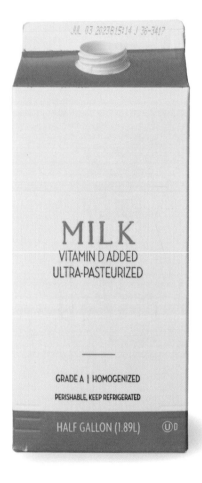

thin cardboard

roof (cut 2)
2 by 3½ inches

corrugated cardboard

A (cut 2)
3¾ by 7 inches

B (cut 1)
3 by 7½ inches

C (cut 2)
3¾ by 3¾ inches

D (cut 2)
3 by 3¾ inches

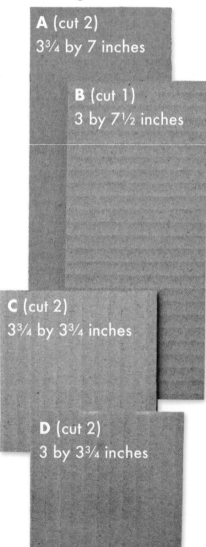

from your toolbox:

craft knife
white glue
hot glue gun
paintbrush
gesso
acrylic craft paint
ruler
scissors
washi tape (or other colored tape)

optional:

pencil with eraser
fabric (4 by 4 inches)

1. Use a craft knife to cut out the spout of the two milk cartons.

2. Glue a cardboard **roof** piece over each hole.

3. Ask a grown-up to hot-glue the two cartons together.

4. Prime with the gesso and then paint with acrylic craft paint.

5. With a grown-up's help, use the knife and ruler to cut down the center and top and bottom edges of each milk carton, following the red dashed line, to create doors.

6. To create a second-floor bedroom, measure halfway up the dividing wall between the milk cartons. Draw a line. Next draw a line at the top edge of the wall. Cut along the two drawn lines with scissors.

7. Ask a grown-up to run a craft knife along the crease on the upper part of the back wall to cut it out.

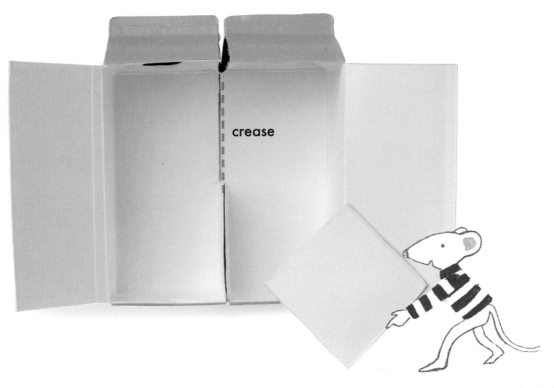

crease

8. Paint the two **A** pieces and the **B** piece white.

9. Glue in the **A** pieces (bedroom ceiling and floor). Now you are ready to decorate your house!

A

A

B

A

bedroom

A

10. Make piece **B** a striped wall with washi tape. (Use a small piece of washi tape as a spacer guide, moving it along after you add each stripe.)

11. Paint the two **C** pieces (living room & kitchen walls) any color you choose. You could also add polka dots by using a new pencil eraser as a stamp. Dip the eraser into a thin layer of paint and stamp it onto the cardboard wall. Or decorate any other way you'd like.

12. One way to decorate the kitchen & living room floors (**D** pieces) is to add fabric. Glue the cardboard to the back of the fabric and then trim any extra fabric.

13. Add masking tape loops to the backs of the walls (the **B** and **C** pieces) and floors (the **D** pieces), and then press them into place.

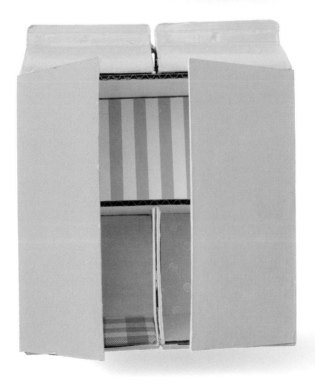

BONUS: See page 110 to turn your Mousehouse into storage for your little crafts and a carrying case.

Craft a Mini Mouse Toy

Pom-poms are the perfect material for a toy mouse that is fuzzy and so cute!
Use the mini size pom-poms to make an itty-bitty toy for Mouse.

pom-poms
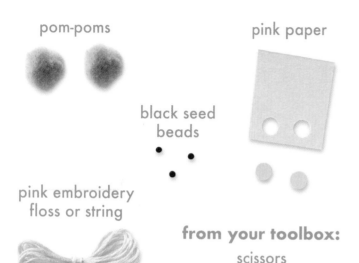
pink paper

black seed
beads

pink embroidery
floss or string

from your toolbox:

scissors
toothpick
white glue
hole punch

1. Glue 2 pom-poms together so they create an oval.

2. **Add eyes and nose:** Use a toothpick to dot glue where you would like the eyes and nose to go and place a bead on those spots. Use the clean end of the toothpick to push the bead into the pom-pom.

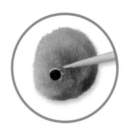
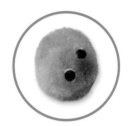

3. Use a hole punch to make 2 pink circles for ears. Add a little glue to one side of each ear and slide them into the pom-pom.

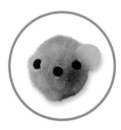

4. **Add a tail:** Use the toothpick to dot glue into the back pom-pom, and push in one end of a short piece of string.

Make Mouse's Bed

Make Mouse's bed and give Mouse a cozy place to sleep.

sponge and fabric (we used felt) for mattress, blanket, and pillow

sardine or anchovy tin

from your toolbox:
super glue gel
pencil
scissors
pinking shears

8 beads:
4 small and
4 medium

1. Glue 2 beads together (one small and one big) for each leg. The larger bead is the top of the leg.

2. Glue the top of the legs to the bottom of the tin, one at each corner.

3. Trace the shape of the tin onto the sponge and fabric. Cut along the line and push both into the tin for a cozy mattress.

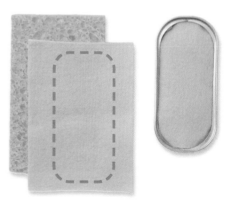

4. Cut a fabric scrap (piece of old towel or clothing) for a blanket and pillow, use pinking shears for a fancy touch.

Make a Matchbox Dresser

Because Mouse can't leave clothes all over the bedroom floor.

small empty matchboxes
(have a grown-up check that they're empty)

rubber bands

medium beads

small beads

from your toolbox:
white glue
toothpick

1. Glue 3 or 4 matchboxes into a stack. Use rubber bands to hold them together while they dry.

2. When the glue is dry, glue a small bead to the front of each drawer for a drawer pull. Glue 4 medium beads to the bottom for feet.

TIP: Dip a toothpick into glue and use it to apply little blobs for attaching the drawer pull and feet.

Teeny-Tiny Pictures and Frames

What will you put in your tiny picture frames? Little photos or pictures that you draw yourself? Mouse has a whole wall of portraits of relatives, friends, and frenemies (cats!).

small jar caps, bottle caps, or buttons

small pictures to frame

matchboxes or jewelry boxes

baker's twine or string

wooden coffee stirrer

from your toolbox:

scissors
glue stick
white glue
clear tape
pencil

1. Trace the frame around the picture and then cut inside the line so that it will fit into the frame.

2. Apply a glue stick to the back of the picture and press it inside the frame.

3. Make a hanger for the frame: Cut a short piece of string, around 3 inches. Fold it in half. Use clear tape or glue to stick both ends of the string to the back of the frame.

BONUS: Cut a wooden coffee stirrer into 4 equal pieces. Glue them together to make a square frame, leaving a little overlap at the corners. Glue a picture to the back of the frame.

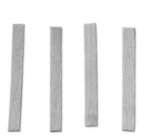

30

Chapter 2: Mouse Goes to Town

Build a Tiny Town

The brightest, tiniest recycled town.

Containers from your recycling bin will make great buildings.
Double-sided tape will help stick on cardboard windows and
doors. Glue on straws for roof details and chimneys.

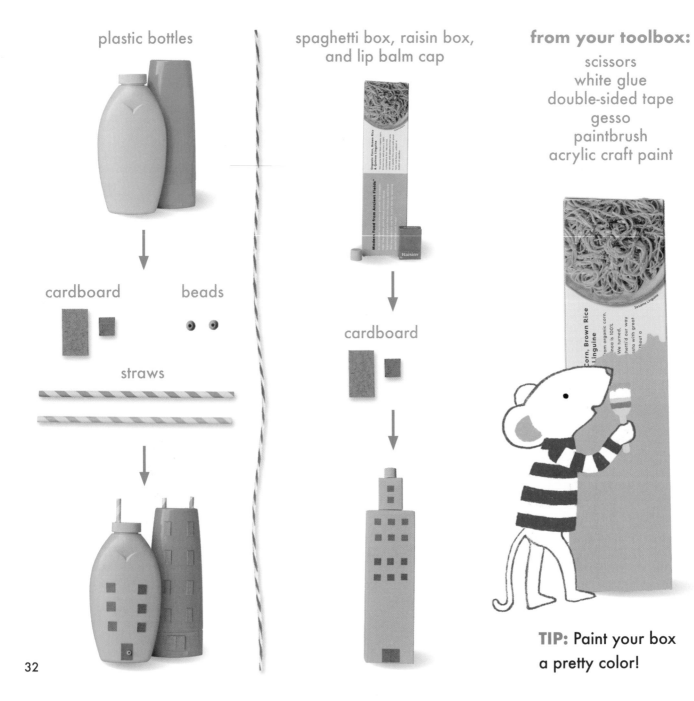

plastic bottles

cardboard   beads

straws

spaghetti box, raisin box,
and lip balm cap

cardboard

from your toolbox:

scissors
white glue
double-sided tape
gesso
paintbrush
acrylic craft paint

TIP: Paint your box
a pretty color!

Make a Candy Store

Every town needs a candy store!

milk carton	wide craft sticks	raisin box	cardboard windows & doors	pipe cleaners	from your toolbox:

milk carton

wide craft sticks

sticker letters

raisin box

cardboard windows & doors

pipe cleaners

from your toolbox:
scissors
gesso
paintbrush
acrylic craft paint
white glue

1¾-inch dowels

bead

1. Cut off the bottom 4 inches of the milk carton and cut out the spout. Gesso and then paint the top part of the milk carton, raisin box, and door.

2. Paint the craft sticks, 2 in one color and 2 in another. Once they are dry, cut them in half.

3. Glue on the raisin box entrance, door, windows, bead doorknob, and roof sticks. Add the sticker letters.

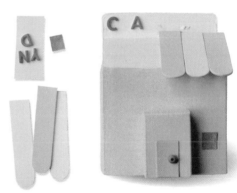

4. Make lollipops: Twist 2 different-colored pipe cleaners together and then coil them into a circle. Repeat and then glue the circles to the dowels. Glue them behind the rooftop, as shown on page 30.

34

Littlest Library

Which tiny book will you check out?

from your toolbox:

scissors
paintbrush
acrylic craft paint
white glue
double-sided tape

library building:

Cut out and paint 2 small rectangles for the door and window. Glue a bead doorknob onto the door. Use double-sided tape to stick them to the container, and add sticker letters.

recycled wide plastic container with lid

sticker letters

cardboard window & door

bead

giant book:

Paint the cardboard book cover. Fold the cover and stack of paper in half. Glue the papers together at the center fold and then to the center fold of the cover.

cardboard & newspaper, cut to the same size

shrub:

Cut a cupcake paper in half. Bring the ends of the cut side together and overlap them to form a cone. Add glue under the overlap.

cupcake paper

Milk Stand

Mouse can't make Ginger's favorite cake without milk!

small plastic
milk bottle

craft
stick

straw

carboard, about
1 ¼ inch square,
for window

colored paper, about
1 by 1 ½ inches,
for awning

from your toolbox:
scissors
white glue
adhesive dots
optional:
scalloped paper edger

1. Fold down ½ inch or so along the width of the awning paper. Cut a piece of the craft stick just a bit wider than the width of the awning paper.

OPTIONAL: Use a scalloped paper edger to cut a scalloped edge.

2. Glue the awning to the top of the cardboard and the craft stick "counter" to the bottom.

3. Use adhesive dots to stick the window to the bottle and add a 1-inch piece of straw chimney to the top of the cap.

BONUS: Use the same steps to make a lemonade stand using a lemon juice bottle.

Make a Wagon

The best way to get around Mousetown!

bottle caps

anchovy or sardine tin, painted if you like

cardboard

nickel

from your toolbox:
ruler
pencil
scissors
adhesive dots
white glue
optional:
paintbrush
acrylic craft paint

wooden skewer

straws

1. Make the axles: Cut a straw into 2 pieces that are about ½ inch wider than the tin. Cut the skewer into 2 pieces ½ inch longer than the straw pieces. Save the pointy end of the skewer.

2. Use adhesive dots to stick the straws to the bottom of the tin.

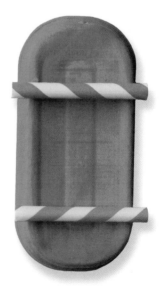

3. Trace the nickel 4 times on the cardboard. Use the pointy end of the skewer to poke a hole in the center of each cardboard circle.

6. Slide each skewer into a straw. Squeeze white glue into the holes of the remaining 2 wheels and attach to the end of the skewers.

TIP: Be sure to attach the wheels to the skewers only; that way they can turn freely inside the straw axles.

4. Cut out the 4 circles. Use adhesive dots to stick them to the inside of the bottle caps. These are the wheels.

5. Squeeze white glue into the holes and stick one end of each skewer into a wheel.

7. Make a handle: Cut a 1-inch piece of straw and a 2-inch piece of straw. Glue the short straw across the longer straw in a T shape. Squeeze the bottom of the T to flatten it, and use an adhesive dot to attach it to the front of the wagon.

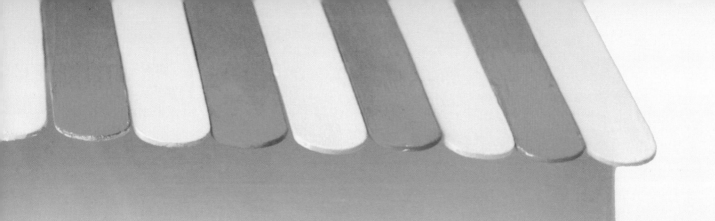

Chapter 3:

At the

BAKERY

Make the Most Petite Pies*

Mouse's bakery needs treats, and pies are a Mousetown favorite!

1 tablespoon (15 ml) softened butter

6–8 bottle caps

berries

1½ graham crackers

small leaves of mint or other herb

1. **Crush graham crackers into crumbs. Use a spoon to mix the butter with the crumbs.**

2. **Press a little of the crumb mixture into a bottle cap and push down the middle to make a well.**

3. **Top with a berry and a mini mint leaf— the inside leaf of a mint sprig.**

*With your grown-up mouse's permission you can snack on these ingredients while you work! But once the crumbs are in the bottle cap, don't eat the pies.

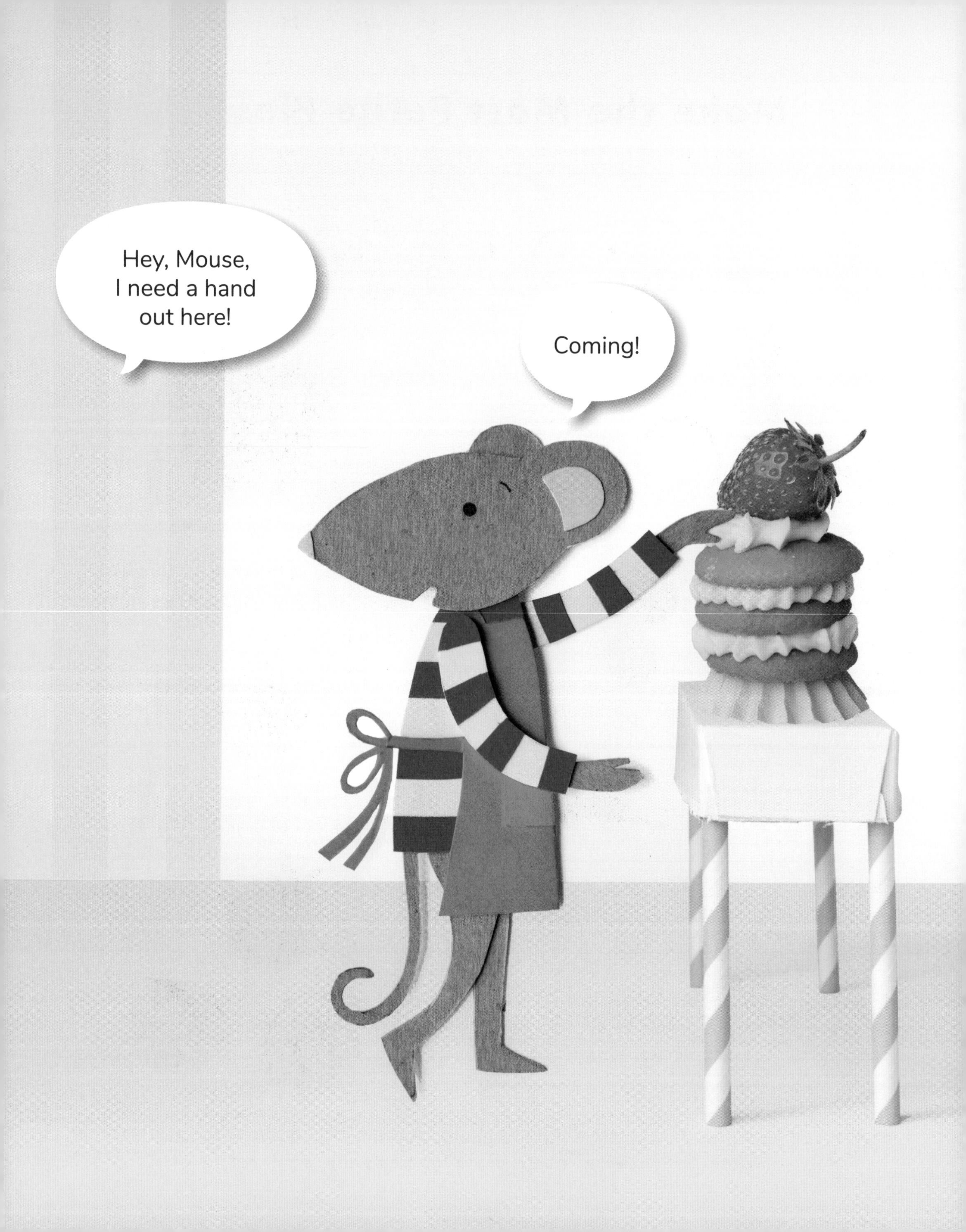
Hey, Mouse,
I need a hand
out here!
Coming!

Craft the Cutest Cakes*

Make mouse-sized cakes with cookies and candy!

Using a tube of frosting as glue, stick cookies and candy together to make tiny cakes. For the marshmallow cake, spread frosting around the sides of the marshmallow and roll it in sprinkles.

mini sandwich cookies

+

sprinkle

=

marshmallow

+

large round sprinkles

+

heart sprinkle

=

wafer candy

+

marshmallow rainbow

=

vanilla wafers

+

large round sprinkle

=

*Check with your grown-up mouse before eating any crafts.

Make Mini Marshmallow Ice Cream Cones*

Finally, ice cream cones that don't drip!

large round sprinkles

mini marshmallows

ice cream cone

from your toolbox:
serrated knife
scissors
toothpick

1. Ask a grown-up to use a serrated knife to gently saw off the bottom inch of an ice cream cone, without pressing the knife down. This will keep it from cracking.

2. Cut a bit off the bottom of a mini marshmallow with scissors to expose the sticky part, and attach it to the mini cone. If the marshmallow doesn't stick, dab the cut side with a drop of water.

3. Use a toothpick to poke a hole on top of the marshmallow to expose sticky part, and stuff a large round sprinkle into the hole.

TIP: Crush the rest of the cone and sprinkle it over real ice cream as a treat for yourself.

*Check with your grown-up mouse before eating any crafts.

48

49

Craft a Bitty Bakery Case

Show off all your mini baked goods!

plastic box from greens container

straws

corrugated cardboard

from your toolbox:

washi tape (or other colored tape)
scissors
pencil
paintbrush
gesso or white paint
white glue

optional:
cupcake papers

1. The plastic tub, turned upside down, will become the "glass case." Decide how big you'd like it to be and use washi tape to make a line showing where to cut the tub.

2. Use scissors to cut down the center of the tape. You can add tape to any edges that are sharp.

3. Make the shelves: Trace the inside of the open end onto the cardboard to make the bottom shelf.

4. Turn the tub upside down and trace the outside of the top of the box to make the top shelf. Trim the shelves down bit by bit until they fit inside the case.

5. Paint the shelves with gesso or white paint.

OPTIONAL: Cut ½-inch strips from the edge of cupcake papers and glue them to the edge of the cardboard shelves for a fancy touch.

6. Add the shelf holders: Cut the straws into 4 pieces to fit the sides of the bakery case. Tape two straws, one toward the bottom and one halfway up the side of the case. Repeat on the other side.

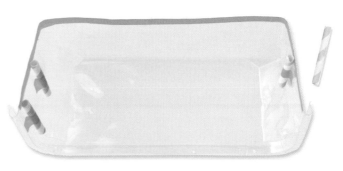

7. Put the shelves into the case and add your desserts.

TIP: Glue one or more straws to the inside top edge and the outside bottom edge for decoration and stability.

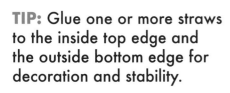

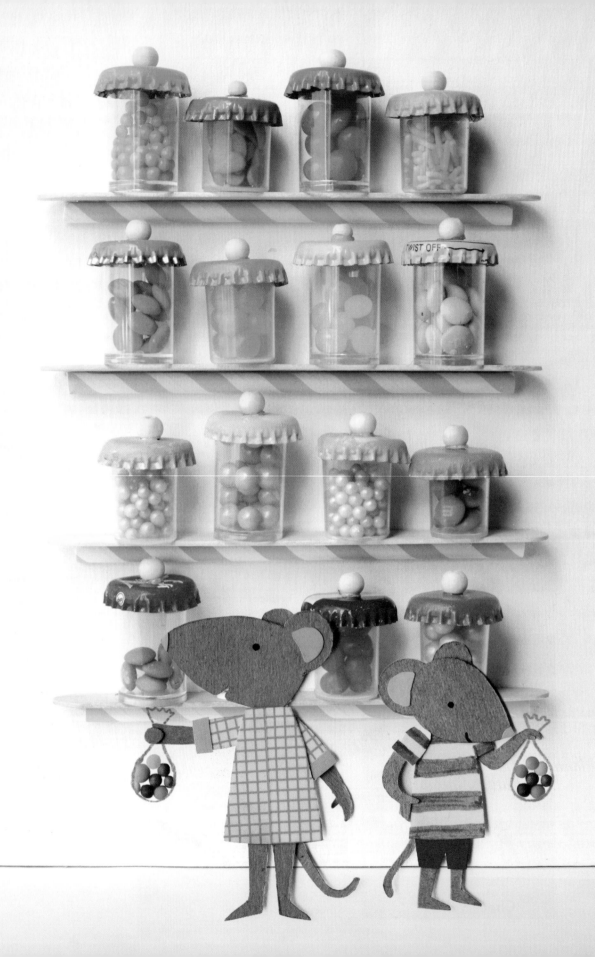

Craft Minuscule Candy Jars*

I'll take one of each, please!

Fill a clear cap with tiny candies or sprinkles.
Make a lid by gluing a bead to the top of a bottle cap.

candy jar

clear
plastic caps

+

bottle caps

+

beads

=

jar fillings

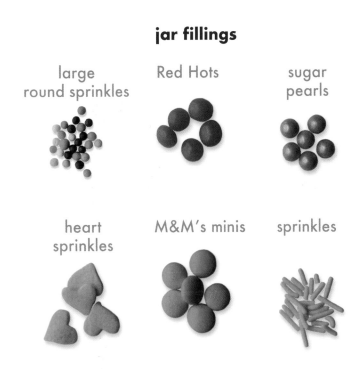

large
round sprinkles

Red Hots

sugar
pearls

heart
sprinkles

M&M's minis

sprinkles

TIPS:

- Caps from spray pump bottles work well as candy jars.
- To preserve these candy jars and keep the candy from spilling out, glue the lids on.
- Colored beads could be substituted for the candy.

*Check with your grown-up mouse before eating any ingredients.

Build Little Cake Stands

Fancy-up your bakery by crafting tiny cake stands to display all your goodies.

Attach the following items together with adhesive dots to make mini cake stands.

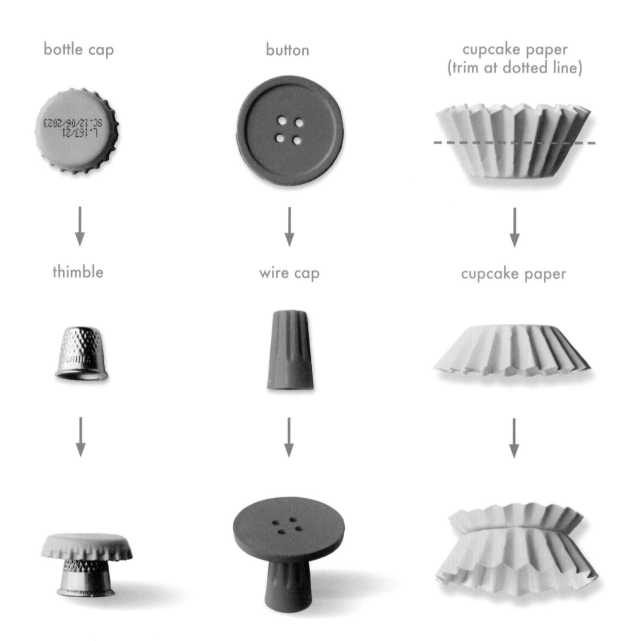

bottle cap	button	cupcake paper (trim at dotted line)
thimble	wire cap	cupcake paper

Make a Ladder

Mouse and Ginger need a way to get to high shelves!

paper straws

from your toolbox:
ruler
scissors
white glue
optional:
wax paper

1. To make ladder rungs (short pieces): Cut a straw into five ¾-inch pieces.

TIP: If you are using a paper straw, the cut ends of straw can get flattened. Pinch to reshape if needed.

2. Cut another straw in half for the side rails.

3. Lay the side rail pieces down. Add glue to both ends of one rung and place between the side rails. Push the pieces together. Repeat with the remaining rungs.

TIP: Do the gluing on a piece of wax paper to protect your table.

TIP: To add a striped wallpaper pattern to your bakery walls, follow the instructions in step 10 on page 22.

56

57

Broom

Time to clean up, Mouse!

straw   toothbrush

from your toolbox:

wire cutters
sandpaper
super glue gel or hot glue
scissors

2. Sand the cut edge of the tooth brush head.

3. Ask a grown-up to help apply super glue gel or hot glue to stick the brush to the straw handle. Trim the straw handle down to the length you'd like.

1. Ask a grown-up to use wire cutters to cut the head off of a toothbrush.

TIP: Ask a grown-up to clean a used toothbrush by washing it with soap and water, dipping it in mouthwash, or boiling it for three minutes.

59

Build a Tiny Shop

*If you change the colors and the details,
it could be a bakery, a mini-mart, or a flower shop!*

empty cereal box with the
top glued shut

clear plastic lid from greens container,
sticker removed (for windows)

wide craft sticks
(around 20)

6 straws for
window frames

corrugated cardboard

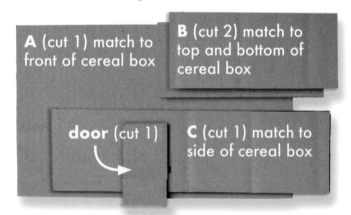

A (cut 1) match to
front of cereal box

B (cut 2) match to
top and bottom of
cereal box

door (cut 1)

C (cut 1) match to
side of cereal box

bead

1 Velcro
dot set

letter stickers

from your toolbox:

paintbrush
gesso
acrylic craft paint
ruler
pencil
craft knife

permanent marker
scissors
white glue
masking tape

1. Prime the box with gesso and paint it.

2. Paint the cardboard pieces white (or any other color you'd like) and the door the same color as the box.

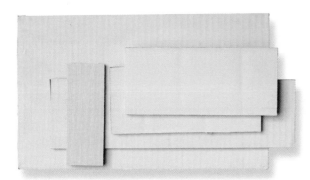

3. Set the box on its side. Measure 1½ inches from the top edge of the box and draw a horizontal line. Find the center of the horizontal line and draw a vertical line to the bottom of the box.

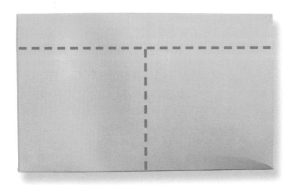

4. Ask a grown-up to use a ruler and craft knife to cut the front of the box open, following your drawn lines and along the bottom to make flaps.

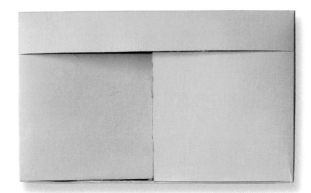

5. Have a grown-up use the ruler and craft knife to cut window holes in the front flaps. (Save a cardboard scrap from one of the windows.)

6. Paint the inside of the front flap white if you'd like.

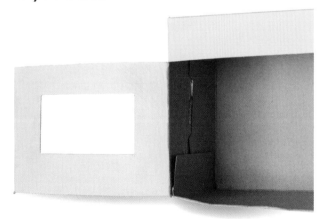

7. Make window panes: Using the permanent marker and one of the cardboard window scraps for size, draw two rectangles about ¼ inch larger all around onto the plastic lid. Cut them out.

8. Glue the window panes behind the window openings and tape them in place while the glue dries. Remove the tape.

OPTIONAL: Use straw pieces to frame the window; glue them in place.

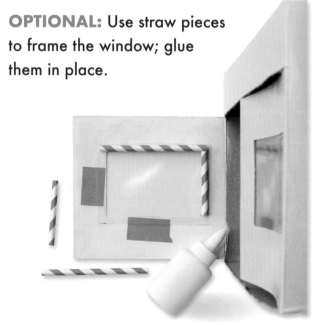

9. Add sticker letters and a straw top to the outside of the window.

10. Use masking tape loops to stick piece **A** (back wall), the two **B** pieces (side walls), and piece **C** (floor) inside the shop.

NOTE: See page 66 to add shelves to the back wall (piece **A**) before placing it in the store.

11. Make an angled roof: Ask a grown-up to use a ruler and craft knife to cut along the red dotted lines on the long side of the box.

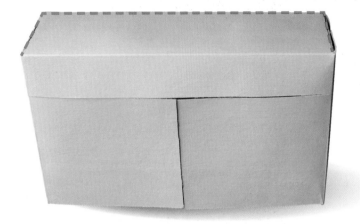

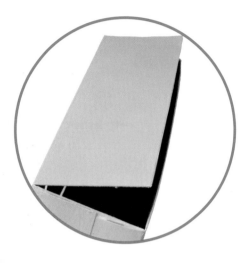

12. Paint one craft stick the color of the box and cut it in half. This is the roof support.

13. Lift up the new flap to make an angled roof. Glue a craft stick support on each side to keep the roof tilted up.

14. Paint half of the remaining sticks one color and the other half another color. Cut a little off the end of each stick.

15. Glue on craft sticks with the straight sides at the top, alternating colors, to make an awning.

16. Center the door over the front seam and glue it to the left flap. Glue on a bead doorknob and use a Velcro dot set to close it.

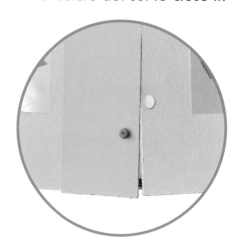

Build A Little Shop Shelf Wall

The perfect place for your cakes and pies!

To make shelves for your shop, remove corrugated cardboard piece **A** (shown on page 63)and follow the instructions below.

A   corrugated cardboard

wide craft sticks

straws

from your toolbox:
ruler
pencil
scissors
white glue
tape

1. **Make shelf supports:** Use a ruler and pencil to draw lines where you would like shelves on the back wall. (Mouse left room for the bakery case; see facing page.) If you need to, trim the straws, and then glue them on the lines.

TIP: Stick your jars to the shelves with an adhesive dot to keep everything in place.

2. Make shelves: While the straw glue dries, trim the rounded edges from craft sticks and cut them as needed, to match the straw shelf supports. Glue the shelves onto the straw supports.

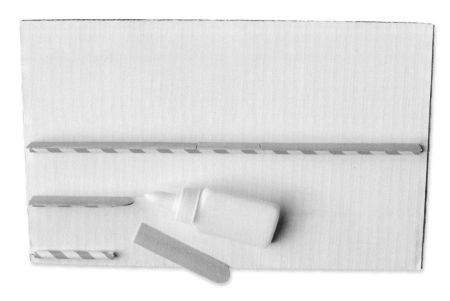

3. Use tape loops to attach the shelf wall to the back wall of the bakery. Add the candy jars, pies, cakes, and anything else you'd like.

EGGS
1.99

MILK
$1

50¢

99¢

**Chapter 4:
Mouse
Goes
Shopping**

TUNA
5/$1.

79

CUPS
$2.29

$1.00

Craft Bitsy Grocery Bags

Another great way to recycle paper!

recycled paper bag cut to 3 by 5 inches

from your toolbox:
white glue
ruler
clear tape
string or twine

1. Fold both sides of the paper in so that it overlaps 1 inch in the center.

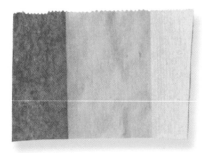

2. Squeeze a thin line of glue under the overlapping edge and press it down.

3. Fold the bottom a ½ inch upward.

4. Glue or tape the folded bottom in place.

5. Cut two 3-inch pieces of twine. Fold a piece of twine in half and tape the ends inside the the top edge of the bag around ¾ inch apart. Repeat on the other side.

6. OPTIONAL: Decorate the bags using stickers, washi tape, rubber stamps, and colored paper, or any other way you'd like!

Make a Tiny Fruit Stand

Mice eat fruits and vegetables too!

6 small boxes
(like lids and bottoms
from jewelry boxes)

corrugated
cardboard

2¾ by 2
inches

from your toolbox:

scissors
white glue

1. Cut the cardboard rectangle in half diagonally to make two triangles.

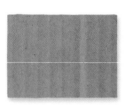

2. Glue the sides of the boxes together to form a rough rectangle. Let it dry.

3. Turn the glued boxes over and glue the long side of the triangle on one side, so that the stand will lean diagonally. Repeat on the other side, making sure the short sides of the triangle are facing the same way.

Make Mini Fruits and Veggies

The tiniest lemons, limes, cucumbers, and oranges!

felt

wooden beads

from your toolbox:
paintbrush
acrylic craft paint
scissors
white glue
optional:
pipe cleaner

1. Choose beads with colors and shapes that make them look like fruits and veggies. You can also paint them a color, or add stripes, like for the watermelon.

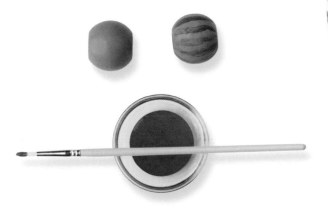

2. Cut out felt leaf shapes and glue them to the beads.

TIP: Slide beads onto a pipe cleaner to paint a bunch of them at once.

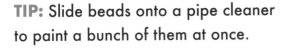

Make Tiny Cans

Make tiny versions of your favorite supermarket products!

corks or spools
(recycled or available
at craft stores)

stickers

thin colored paper

from your toolbox:
scissors
silver acrylic craft paint
paintbrush
washi (or other colored tape)
white glue or glue stick
optional:
sandpaper

1. Cut corks in half. Sand the cut ends smooth if needed.

2. Paint the corks (or spools) silver. These are your cans. Cut strips of paper long enough to wrap around them. These are your labels.

3. Wrap a label around each can and glue or tape the overlap together. Decorate the labels with cut paper shapes, tape stripes, or stickers.

Make Mini Flower Shop Shelves

Bouquets, bouquets, bouquets!

small long box
(like from skin cream)

larger long box
(like from toothpaste)

thimbles and caps from lip
balm and glue stick

various snips of small plants
and wildflowers

small piece
of sponge

from your toolbox:
white glue
paintbrush
gesso
acrylic craft paint
scissors
optional:
gesso

1. Glue the smaller box to one side of the larger box, centered. (Have it hang off the back a bit for a bigger bottom shelf, as Mouse did here.) Allow the glue to dry.

2. Prime the boxes with gesso and then paint the shelves.

3. Add a tiny piece of sponge and then a few drops of water to each vase. Slide a small plant snip or wildflower around the side of the sponge to hold it in place.

TIP: To make your own flower shop, follow the instructions for Build a Tiny Shop on page 60–65. Mouse used a cookie box rather than a cereal box for this flower shop.

TIP: To make balloons: Trace circles onto thin cardboard and cut them out. Glue on a tiny matching triangle and string.

Chapter 5:

Mouse Plans a Party

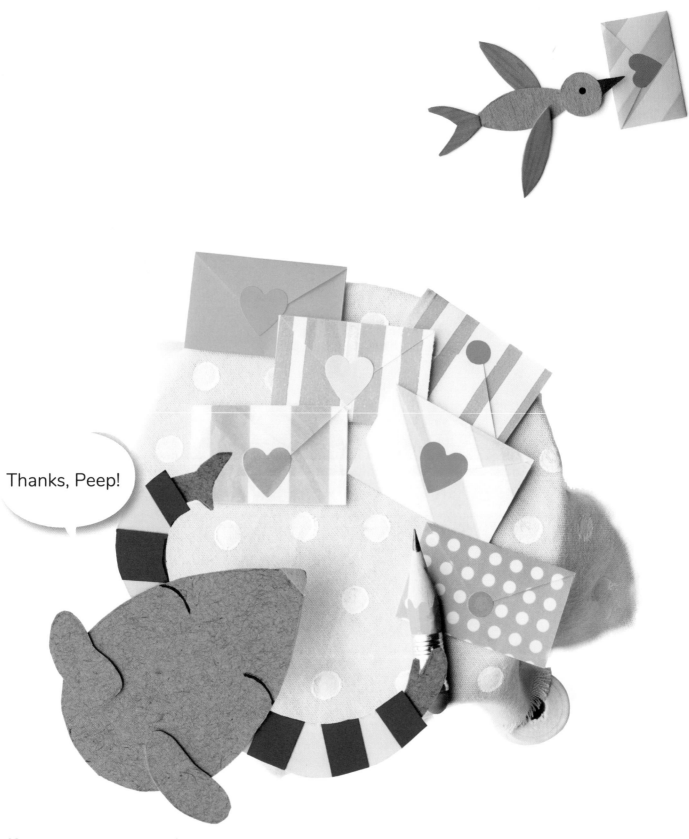

Make Mini Invitations

I wonder who Mouse will invite to Ginger's party?

small stickers

thin scrap paper such as wrapping paper, newspaper, and origami paper

from your toolbox:
pencil
tracing paper
scissors
markers

1. Trace the template onto tracing paper and cut out the card-velope shape.

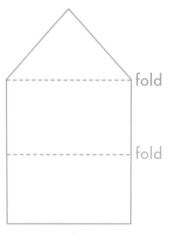

fold

fold

template

2. Fold the card-velope on the dotted lines shown on the template.

3. Lift the flap and write a message on the inside, if you'd like. Refold the bottom flap.

SURPRISE PARTY for GINGER

4. Seal the card-velope with a small sticker.

TIP: To make a polka-dotted tablecloth, decorate a piece of fabric following the instructions in step 11 on page 22.

Craft Bitty Party Hats

What's a party without hats?

jar cap: around 2½ inches wide

thin scrap paper such as wrapping paper, newspaper, and origami paper

beads

from your toolbox:

pencil
scissors
white glue

1. Trace a cap onto a piece of paper. Cut out the circle.

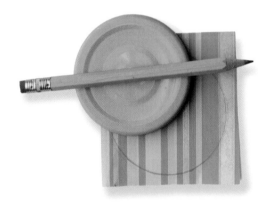

2. Cut the circle in half.

3. Follow the arrows to overlap the two edges of the flat side to form a cone. Glue under the overlap.

4. Decorate the top of the hat using a tiny bead.

Make a Wee Garland

Using recycled paper adds fun color and pattern to Mouse's party decorations!

baker's twine

scrap paper such as maps, paper bags, newspaper, and construction paper

template

from your toolbox:
pencil
tracing paper
scissors
white glue
optional:
wax paper

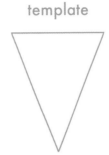

1. Trace the template onto tracing paper and cut it out. Use the template to trace triangles onto different pieces of paper. You'll need about 12 for every 12 inches of garland. Cut the triangles out.

3. Arrange the triangles in the order you'd like upside down on a piece of wax paper (to protect your table), and then glue the string to the top of the triangles.

2. Cut a piece of string as long as you'd like your garland plus an extra inch per side so it can easily hang.

Build Tiny Tables

*Mix and match the tabletops and legs
to make your own unique tiny table!*

spool

jar lid

straws

Cut two straws into
four 3½-inch pieces.

cheese box

beads

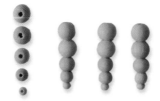

Glue five beads together
to make a leg (a mix of
sizes or all the same).

jewelry box lid

Glue a spool to
the underside of
a cheese box.

Repeat three times.
Glue the legs under the
edge of the jar lid.

Glue one inside each
corner of the box lid.

Build Teeny Chairs

The guests need somewhere to sit!

toilet paper tubes

1. Trace the templates on the next page onto tracing paper. Cut out the shapes.

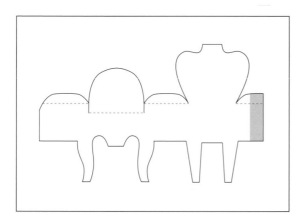

2. Wrap the tracing paper shape around a toilet paper tube and tape it in place.

3. Trace the shape and then cut it out.

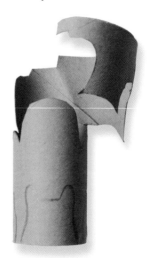

4. Following the dotted lines on the templates, fold down the seat and armrests.

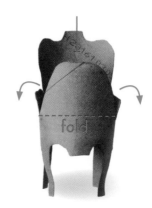

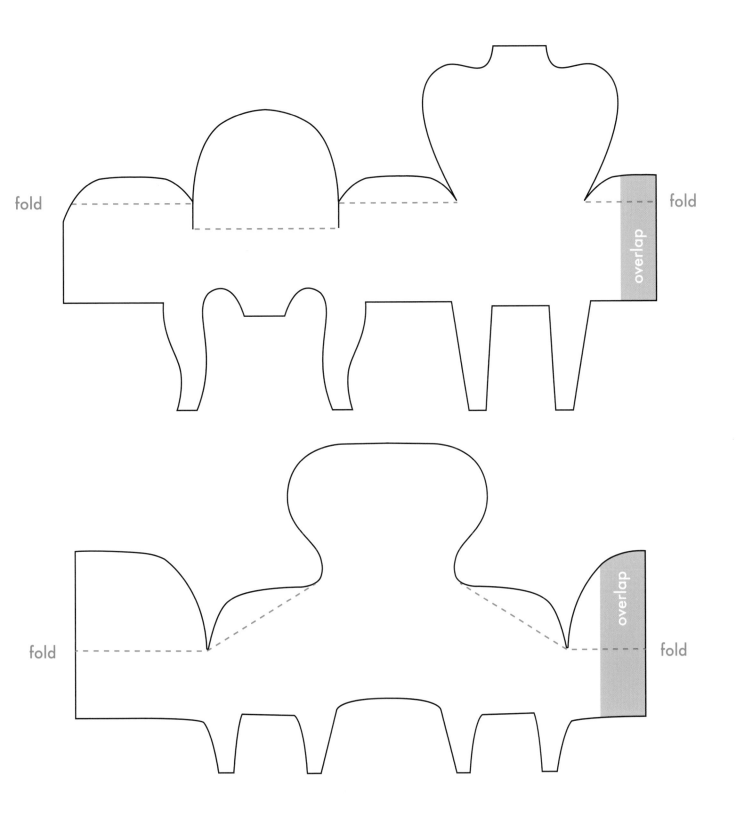

fold

fold

overlap

fold

fold

overlap

Chapter 6: Party Time!

SURPRISE!

Make Lil' Veggies and Dip*

Yes, mice do eat veggies! Even at a party.

Take big veggies and make them mouse-sized by trimming them
down with a kitchen knife. Ask a grown-up for help!

1. Arrange the cucumber slice platter
with veggies and snips of dill or another
herb for garnish.

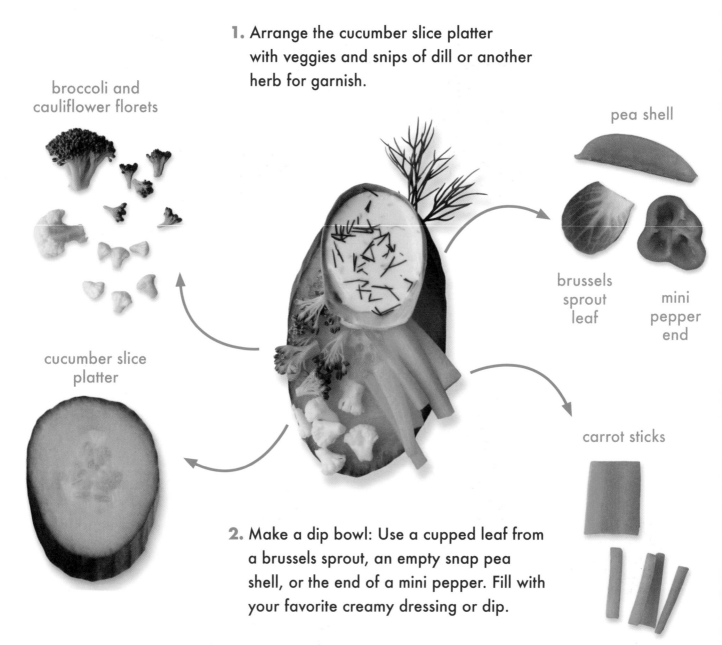

broccoli and
cauliflower florets

pea shell

brussels
sprout
leaf

mini
pepper
end

cucumber slice
platter

carrot sticks

2. Make a dip bowl: Use a cupped leaf from
a brussels sprout, an empty snap pea
shell, or the end of a mini pepper. Fill with
your favorite creamy dressing or dip.

*Check with your grown-up mouse before eating any ingredients.

Craft a Cute Cheese Platter*

*Mice love cheese! Build a bitty cheese board for Ginger's birthday.
Mousetown will thank you!*

Cut meat, cheese, and crackers into a mouse-sized cheese board
using a kitchen knife. Ask a grown-up for help!

cheese

1. Tear a sheet of wax paper to fit your
platter and arrange the cheese and
meat, along with herbs for garnish, on
top of it.

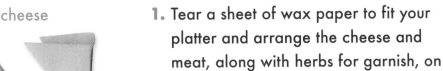

jerky stick—
vegan or meat

large cracker or a wood slice
(available at craft stores)

flour tortillas

2. Cut a flour tortilla into tiny square
crackers. With a grown-up's help, place
on a baking sheet and bake at 350
degrees F (175 degrees C) for 10 minutes
or until lightly golden. When they are
cool, add the crackers to your platter.

*Check with your grown-up mouse before eating any ingredients.

101

Design Dreamy Dainty Drinks*
From shakes to teas to tiny sodas!

Use clean spray bottle caps or thimbles as cups.
Mix and match the ingredients below or invent your own tiny drink.

short shakes

vanilla yogurt +
strawberry yogurt

whipped cream +
chocolate pudding +
large round sprinkle

melted mint ice cream
+ a mint leaf

tiny teas

mint tea + mint leaf

pink tea (raspberry or
hibiscus) + raspberry

iced tea +
rosemary sprig

small sodas

grape juice + seltzer
+ blueberry

lemonade + seltzer
+ basil leaf

cranberry juice +
seltzer + lemon slice

*Check with your grown-up mouse before eating or drinking any crafts.

Make Miniature Gifts

What's a party without presents?

scrap paper such as maps,
paper bags, newspaper,
and origami paper

small boxes: jewelry
boxes, raisin boxes,
or matchboxes

from your toolbox:
scissors
clear tape
twine, yarn, or string

1. Lay a box on top of the paper and cut the paper so that it is large enough to wrap around with a little overlap.

2. Wrap the paper around the box and tape in place.

3. Fold down one end of the paper and crease on the left and right sides.

4. Fold the left and right sides into the middle to make a triangle.

5. Bring the triangular piece up and tape it in place. Repeat on the other side.

6. Tie some twine, yarn, or string around the box, and knot and trim it.

TIP: If you use newspaper, paint it a pretty color first!

Metric Conversion Chart

Inches	Rounded Metric				
¼	6 mm / .6 cm	4¼	10.8 cm	8¼	21 cm
½	1.3 cm	4½	11.4 cm	8½	21.6 cm
¾	1.9 cm	4¾	12 cm	8¾	22.2 cm
1	2.5 cm	5	12.7 cm	9	22.9 cm
1¼	3.2 cm	5¼	13.3 cm	9¼	23.5 cm
1½	3.8 cm	5½	14 cm	9½	24.1 cm
1¾	4.4 cm	5¾	14.6 cm	9¾	24.8 cm
2	5.1 cm	6	15.2 cm	10	25.4 cm
2¼	5.7 cm	6¼	15.9 cm	10¼	26 cm
2½	6.4 cm	6½	16.5 cm	10½	26.7 cm
2¾	7 cm	6¾	17.1 cm	10¾	27.3 cm
3	7.6 cm	7	17.8 cm	11	27.9 cm
3¼	8.3 cm	7¼	18.4 cm	11¼	28.6 cm
3½	8.9 cm	7½	19 cm	11½	29.2 cm
3¾	9.5 cm	7¾	19.7 cm	11¾	30 cm
4	10.2 cm	8	20.3 cm	12	30.5 cm

Wait, there's one more thing on the next page!

TIP: To make a tiny sign, glue alphabet pasta onto a small piece of cardboard and color the letters with paint pens or markers.

Mousehouse Carrying Case

The perfect place to stash your tiny creations!

NOTE: Start with the Mousehouse you made on page 18.

thin cardboard

A 7½ inches by 1½ inches

B 7½ inches by ½ inch

windows:
½ inch by ¾ inch

6 wide
craft sticks

7-inch-long
ribbon

from your toolbox

scissors
paintbrush
acrylic craft paint
white glue

2 beads

3 Velcro
dot sets

door:
1¾ inches
by 2 inches

1. Paint the cardboard strips and door to match the house. Glue bead doorknobs in place.

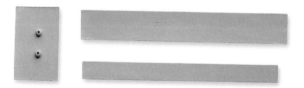

2. Center the wider cardboard strip (**A**) on the opening of the house and glue the left half to the left flap. Glue on the windows.

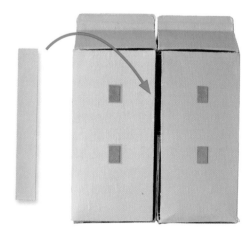

3. Center the door over the front seam and glue only the left half to the left flap. Add Velcro dot sets to attach it to the right side.

4. Use scissors to cut 2½ inches off both ends of the craft sticks. Paint 3 sticks white and the other 3 sticks another color.

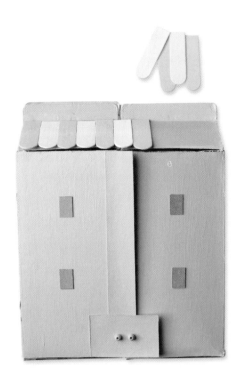

5. Glue craft sticks to the roof with the straight sides at the top, alternating colors. If you like, paint the top strip to match the roof sticks.

7. Add a Velcro dot set to the top left corner of the left flap to make sure it stays closed.

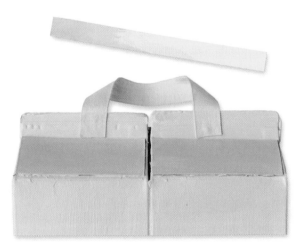

6. Glue the ribbon handle onto the back of the carton tops. Glue the remaining cardboard strip (**B**) on top of the carton tops to sandwich it closed.

Special Thanks

Mousetown is an idea we have been playing around with for several years, and boy are we happy to have been able to make it into a book.

Mousetown owes *quite a bit* to the following people:

Melissa Farris for bringing *Mousetown* to Union Square, for your smart and thoughtful design help, and for answering infinite questions about InDesign. Ardyce Alspach, our editor, for helping us shape our ideas into a real book, keeping us on track with deadlines, and providing lots of encouragement. Your cheerleading meant the world to us! Amelia Mack for getting us across the finish line with wise design guidance as the book made its way through many rounds of proofs. Grace House for her incredible eye for detail and keeping our how-to text consistent and readable. And big thanks to Erika Lusher, Tracey Keevan, and the whole team at Union Square & Co.

Thank you to our agent, Erica Rand Silverman (and the whole Stimola team) for providing invaluable support and advice as we dove into this book. And many thanks to our friends Andy Ward and Jenny Rosenstrach, as well as Meredith Kaffel Simonoff for thoughtful advice and connections.

For early support, we thank Melanie Hoopes and your LRH Memorial Retreat and our fellow retreatees, Susan, Melissa, Molly, Barbara, and the many awe-inspiring sights of that weekend. (Molly!)

For the encouragement and inspiration, we thank: Martha Stewart and the whole MSLO family, Todd Oldham, Deb Bishop, Noel Claro, Kiera Coffee, Carla Glasser, Gabrielle Blair, Jordan Ferney, Amanda Kingloff, Rachel Faucett, Brittany Jepsen, and Seth and Helene Godin.

Thanks to all our friends who listened to lots of mouse talk, looked at artwork, and gave encouragement and feedback, including Amy, Annette, Johanna, Melissa, Page, Simone, Silke, Sophie, Andrea, Ginger (the original Ginger!), Evelyn, and Joyce. And special thanks to Devlin Resetar, for expert photo advice, and Lily (employee #1), for top-notch Photoshop skills.

And most especially to our families who gave us the time, space, and energy to work on this project:

Margaret:

Jeff, thanks for your support and love, and for being a tireless sounding board for all ideas and an incredible resource for all story and writing questions. Thanks to my parents, Jack and Marion, for their enthusiastic support of me and my artwork, and thanks to Felix for all your help and for making me laugh.

Jodi:

Thank you to Fred, my love and partner in all things, and biggest supporter. I am grateful for your science-y brain and artist's-eye for the best advice and feedback. Thank you to my sweet boys, Sammy and Lionel, I'm the luckiest mom! For a lifetime of support and encouragement thank you to my parents, Adele and Sheldon. Thanks to my mother-in-law RoseMary; siblings David, Mary, Allison, Kat, and Greg; nephews and nieces; and my whole family!